PHONICS PRACTICE BOOK

Kindergarten

Orlando   Boston   Dallas   Chicago   San Diego

Visit The Learning Site!
www.harcourtschool.com

CONTENTS

Name_____

Mm

Have children name and trace the letter Mm at the top of the page. Ask them to find and mark the letter Mm in the mittens.

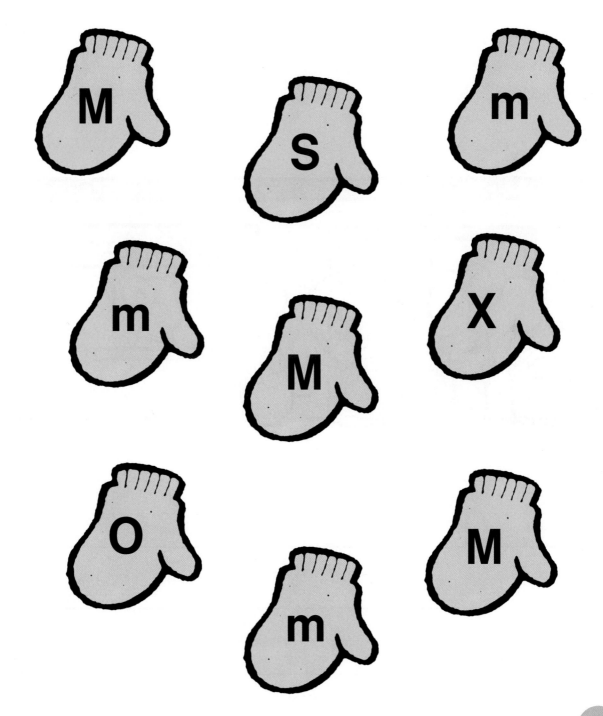

© Harcourt

Name_____

Have children print Mm on the movie sign. Then ask them to trace and write M and m on the lines.

© Harcourt

Name_____

Mm

Have children name each picture and color the items whose names begin with the /m/ sound, as in *mouse*.

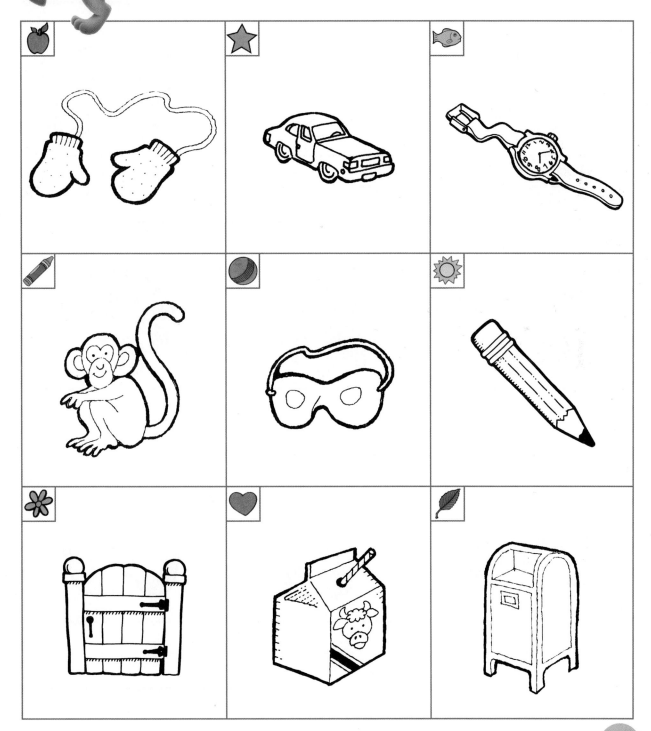

Name_____

Ask children to listen for the beginning sound as you say the name of each picture. Have children write M or m on the lines if the picture name begins with the letter Mm.

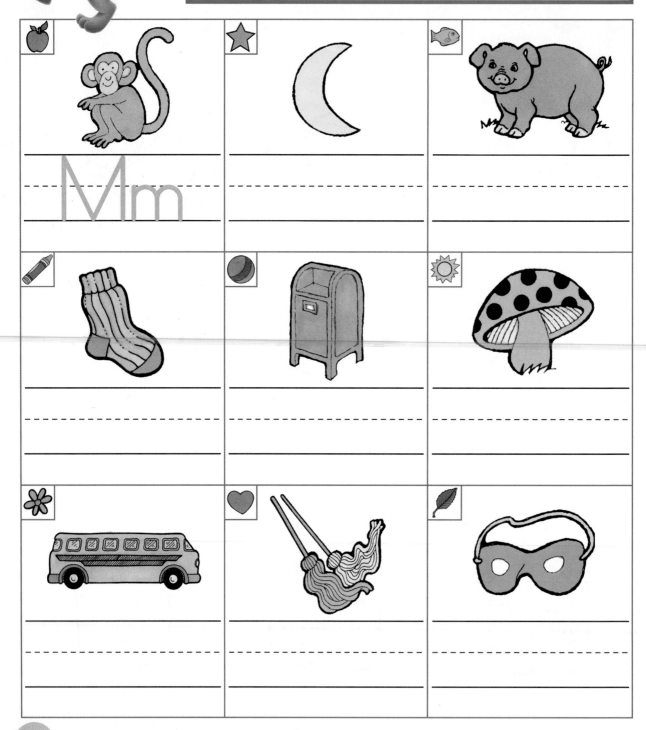

© Harcourt

Ss

Have children name and trace the letter Ss at the top of the page. Ask them to find and mark the letter Ss in the socks.

Phonics Practice Book

Consonant /s/s

9

Name

Have children print Ss on the sandwich truck. Then ask them to trace and write S and s on the lines.

Sandwiches

Soup

SS   ss

SS   ss

Name_____

Ss

Have children name each picture and color the items whose names begin with the /s/ sound, as in *seal*.

Name _____

Ss

Ask children to listen for the beginning sound as you say the name of each picture. Have children write S or s on the lines if the picture name begins with the letter Ss.

Name_____

Rr

Have children name and trace the letter Rr at the top of the page. Ask them to find and mark the letter Rr in the rings.

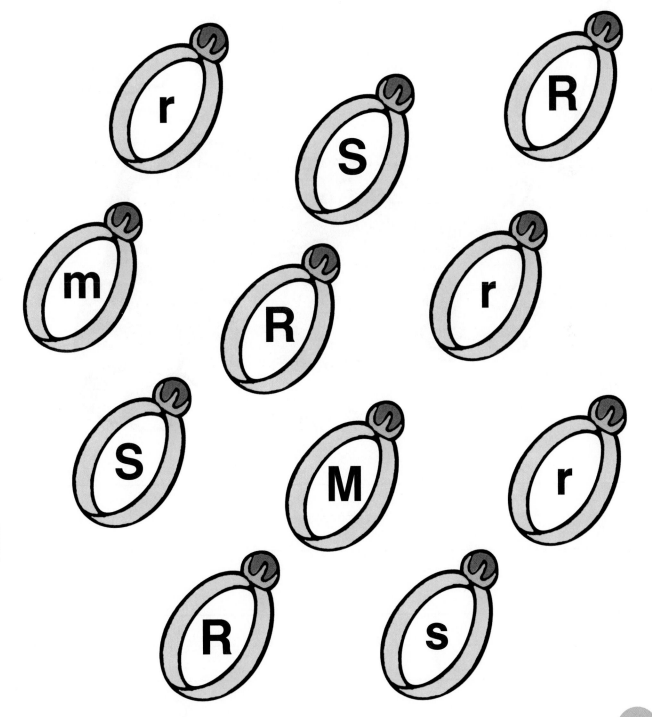

Name_____

RR   rr

RR   rr

© Harcourt

Name_____

Rr

Have children name each picture and color the items whose names begin with the /r/ sound, as in *rabbit*.

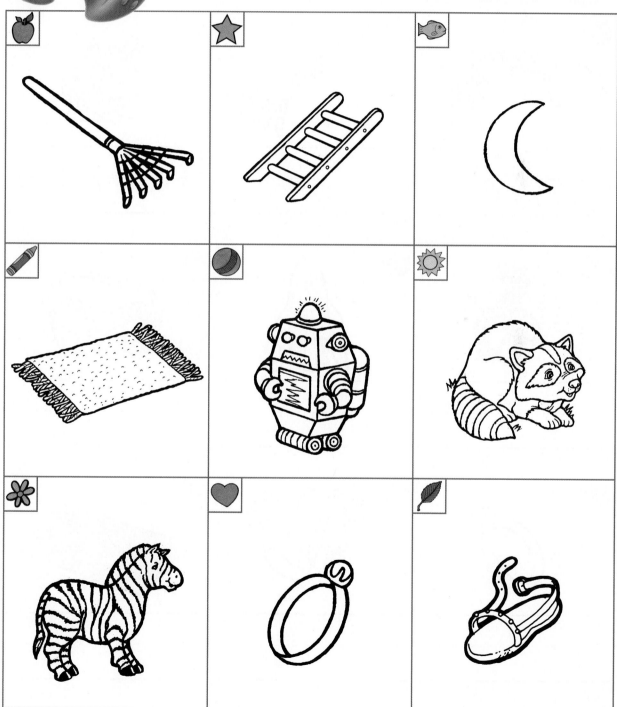

Consonant /r/r   15

Name _____

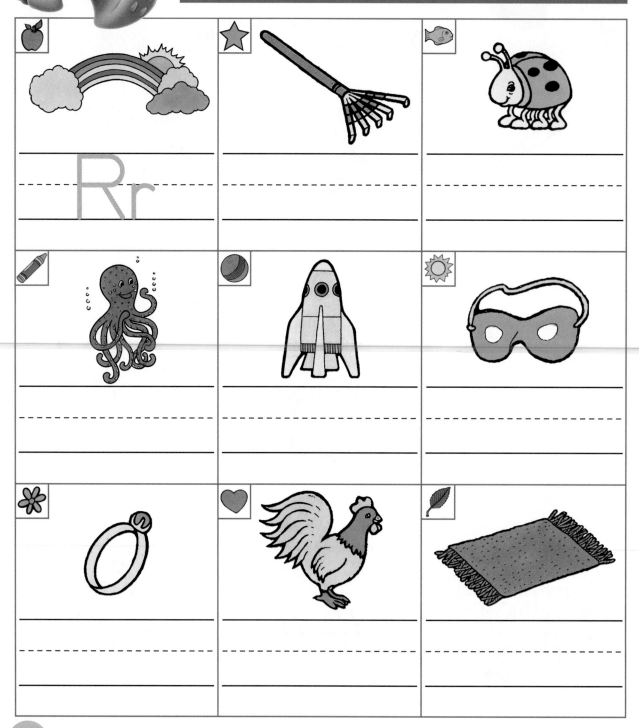

Ask children to listen for the beginning sound as you say the name of each picture. Have children write R or r on the lines if the picture name begins with the letter Rr.

Rr

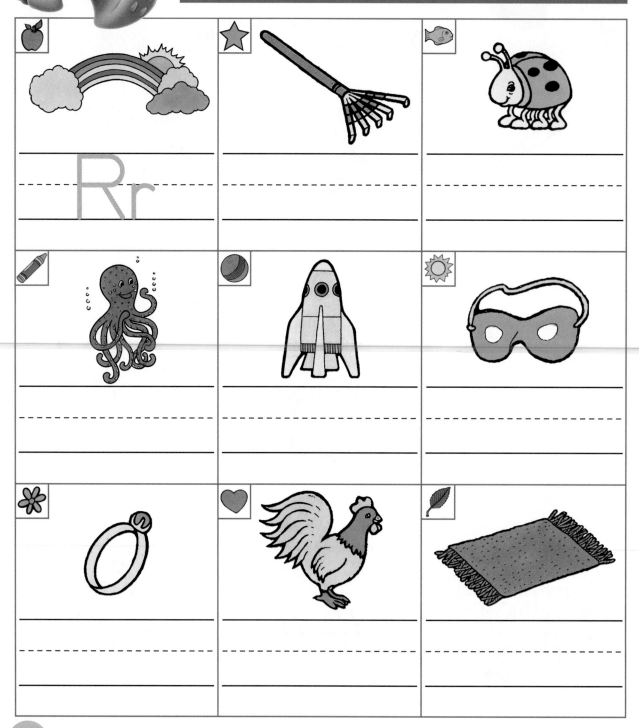

© Harcourt

Name _____

T t

Have children name and trace the letter Tt at the top of the page. Ask them to find and mark the letter Tt in the tops.

© Harcourt

Name_____

Tiger Tom Is Ten Today!

Name _____

Tt

Have children name each picture and color the items whose names begin with the /t/ sound, as in *turtle*.

Name _____

Tt

Ask children to listen for the beginning sound as you say the name of each picture. Have children write T or t on the lines if the picture name begins with the letter Tt.

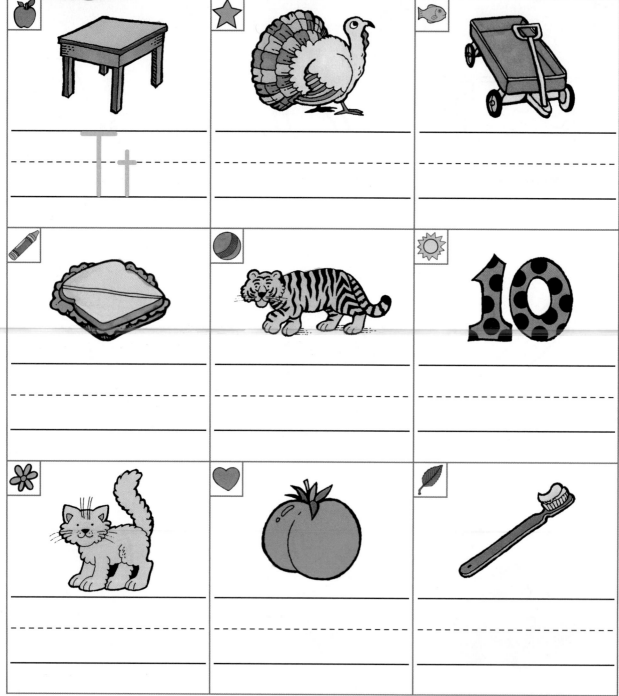

Consonant /t/t

© Harcourt

Name _____

Say the name of each picture. Then have children circle the letter that stands for its beginning sound.

r   t   m

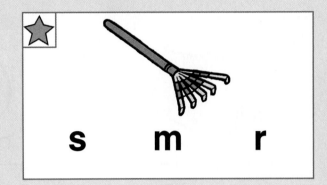

s   m   r

r   s   t

s   t   m

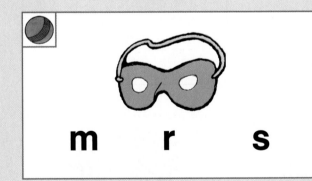

m   r   s

m   s   r

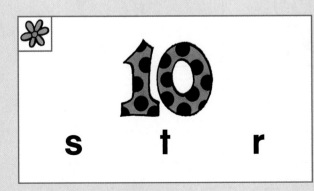

s   t   r

s   t   m

Name_____

Say the name of each picture. Then have children write the letter that stands for its beginning sound.

_____

_____

_____

_____

_____

_____

_____

_____

_____

© Harcourt

Name_____

Pp

Have children name and trace the letter Pp at the top of the page. Ask them to find and mark the letter Pp in the pumpkins.

Name_____

Have children print Pp on the pet store sign. Then ask them to trace and write P and p on the lines.

Name_____

Pp

Have children name each picture and color the items whose names begin with the /p/ sound, as in *penguin*.

Name_____

Pp

Ask children to listen for the beginning sound as you say the name of each picture. Have children write P or p on the lines if the picture name begins with the letter Pp.

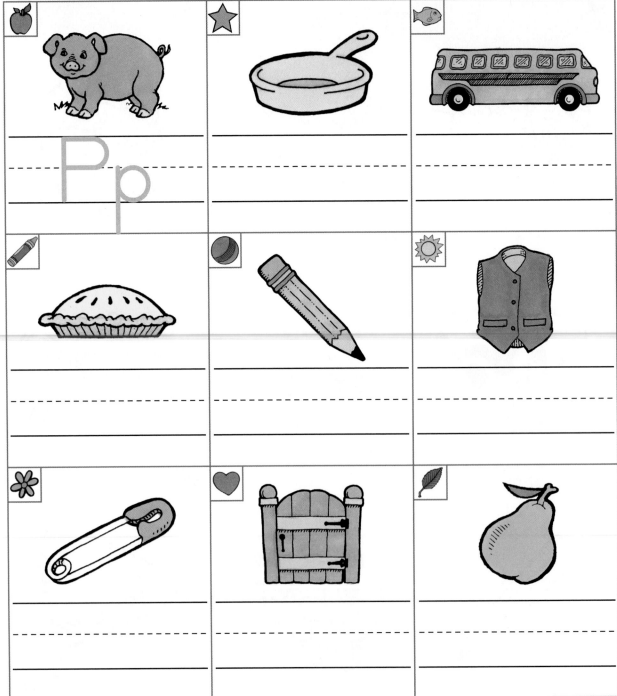

© Harcourt

Name_____

Cc

Have children name and trace the letter Cc at the top of the page. Ask them to find and mark the letter Cc in the cups.

Name _____

© Harcourt

Name _____

Cc

Have children name each picture and color the items whose names begin with the /k/ sound, as in *cat*.

Name_____

Cc

Ask children to listen for the beginning sound as you say the name of each picture. Have children write C or c on the lines if the picture name begins with the letter Cc.

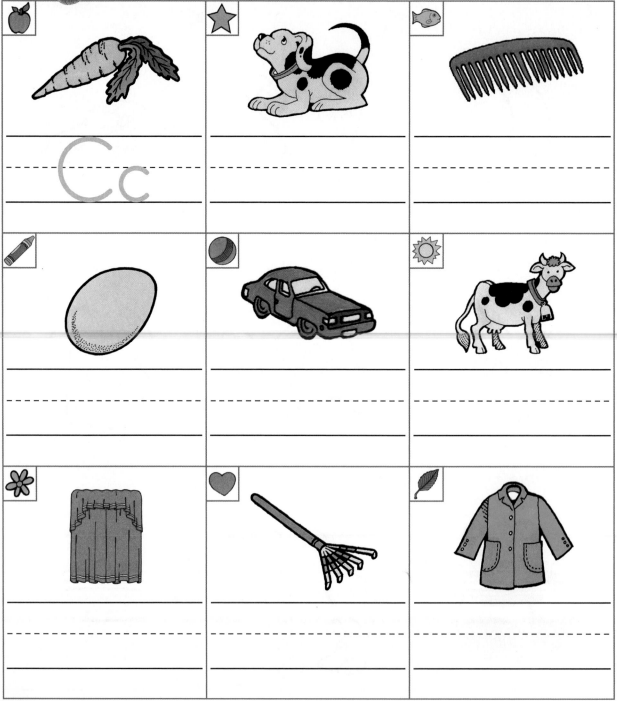

© Harcourt

Name_____

Aa

Have children name and trace the letter Aa at the top of the page. Ask them to find and mark the letter Aa in the apples.

Name_____

Have children print Aa on the apple stand sign. Then
ask them to trace and write A and a on the lines.

Apples
for Sale

Ann's
Apple Pies

AA   aa

AA   aa

© Harcourt

Name _____

Aa

Have children name each picture and color the items whose names begin with the /a/ sound, as in *alligator*.

Name_____

Aa

Ask children to listen for the beginning sound as you say the name of each picture. Have children write A or a on the lines if the picture name begins with the letter Aa.

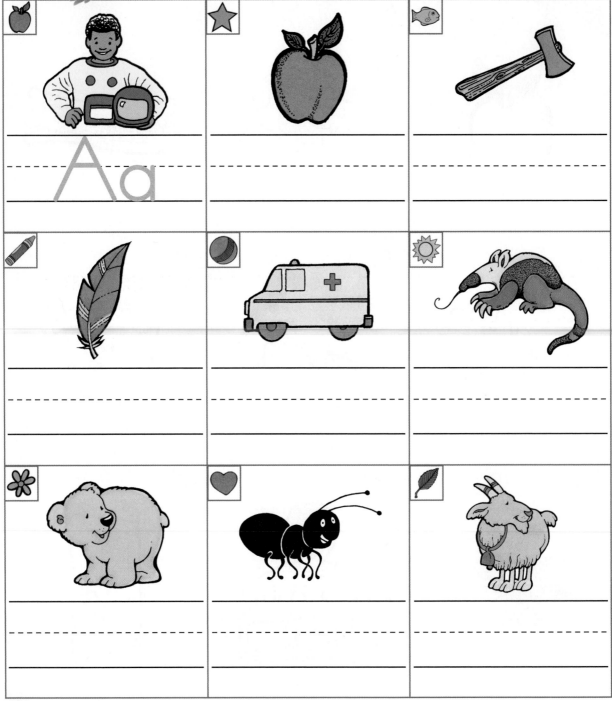

Vowel /a/*a*

Phonics Practice Book

© Harcourt

Name _____

Say the name of each picture. Then have children circle the letter that stands for its beginning sound.

p   c   a

s   a   r

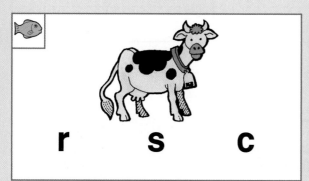

r   s   c

p   t   m

a   r   s

m   p   a

s   p   c

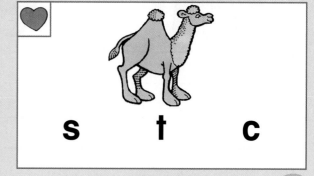

s   t   c

Name _____

Say the name of each picture. Then have children write the letter that stands for its beginning sound.

Review *p, c, a*

Phonics Practice Book

Name _____

Nn

Have children name and trace the letter Nn at the top of the page. Ask them to find and mark the letter Nn in the nests.

Have children print Nn at the top of the newspaper.
Then ask them to trace and write N and n on the lines.

Nickel News 5¢

Nan the Nurse

NN   nn

NN   nn

      Phonics Practice Book

Name_____

Nn

Have children name each picture and color the items whose names begin with the /n/ sound, as in *newt*.

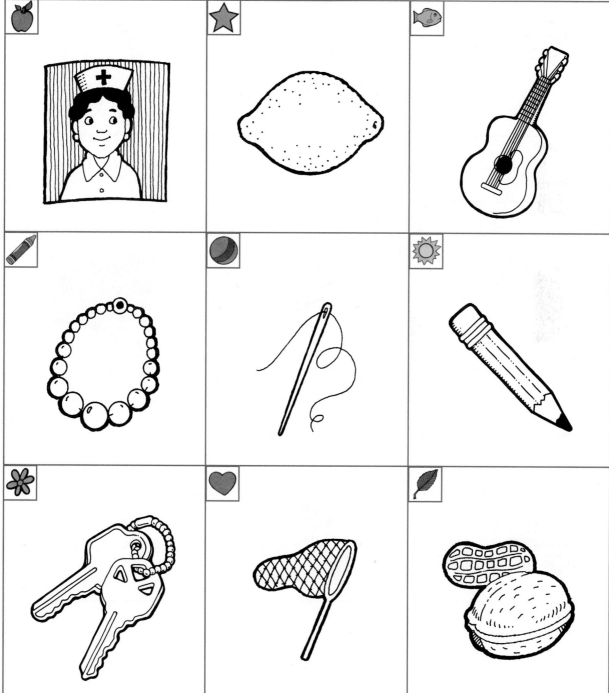

Name _____

Nn

Ask children to listen for the beginning sound as you say the name of each picture. Have children write N or n on the lines if the picture name begins with the letter Nn.

Consonant /n/n

Phonics Practice Book

© Harcourt

Name_____

Dd

Have children name and trace the letter Dd at the top of the page. Ask them to find and mark the letter Dd in the dinosaurs.

 N

 d

 D

 d

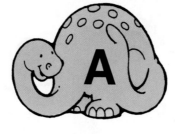 A

 c

 t

 D

 d

 r

 D

© Harcourt

Name_____

Have children print Dd on the dinosaur exhibit sign.
Then ask them to trace and write D and d on the lines.

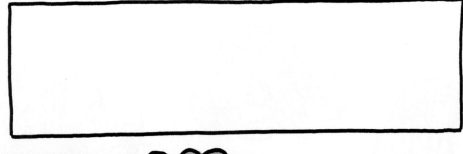

Dinosaurs

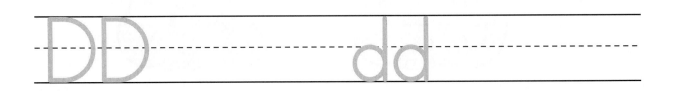

© Harcourt

Name _____

Dd

Have children name each picture and color the items whose names begin with the /d/ sound, as in *duck*.

© Harcourt

Name _____

Dd

Ask children to listen for the beginning sound as you say the name of each picture. Have children write D or d on the lines if the picture name begins with the letter Dd.

Name_____

Say the name of each picture. Then have children circle the letter that stands for its beginning sound.

n   **t**   **d**

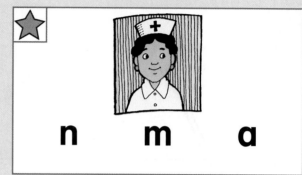

n   **m**   **a**

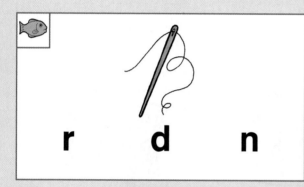

r   **d**   **n**

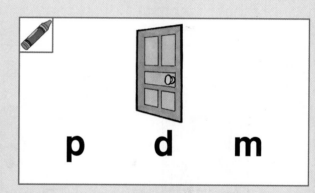

p   **d**   **m**

c   **n**   **s**

n   **d**   **a**

s   **t**   **d**

d   **n**   **r**

Name_____

Say the name of each picture. Then have children write the letter that stands for its beginning sound.

_____

_____

_____

_____

_____

_____

_____

_____

_____

Phonics Practice Book

Name _____

Gg

Have children name and trace the letter Gg at the top of the page. Ask them to find and mark the letter Gg in the gates.

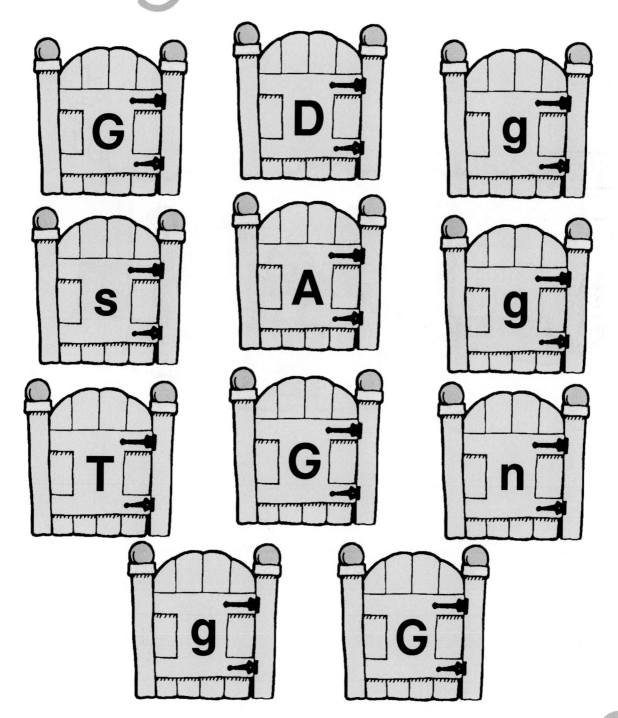

Name_____

Have children print Gg above the garage sale. Then ask
them to trace and write G and g on the lines.

G G   g g

G G   g g

© Harcourt

Name _____

Gg

Have children name each picture and color the items whose names begin with the /g/ sound, as in *goose*.

Name_____

Gg

Ask children to listen for the beginning sound as you say the name of each picture. Have children write G or g on the lines if the picture name begins with the letter Gg.

Name _____

Ff

Have children name and trace the letter Ff at the top of the page. Ask them to find and mark the letter Ff in the fish.

Name_____

Have children print Ff on the banner flying over the farm. Then ask them to trace and write F and f on the lines.

© Harcourt

Name_____

Ff

Have children name each picture and color the items whose names begin with the /f/ sound, as in *fish*.

Name_____

Ff

Ask children to listen for the beginning sound as you say the name of each picture. Have children write F or f on the lines if the picture name begins with the letter Ff.

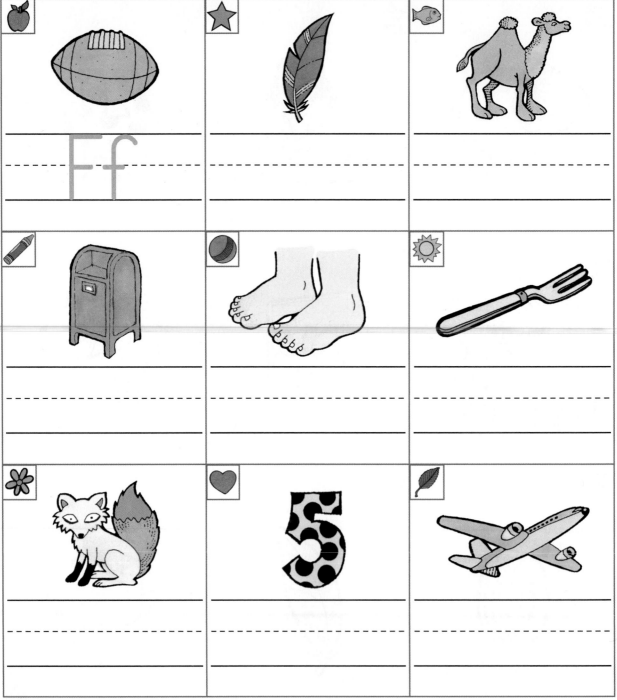

© Harcourt

Name_____

I i

 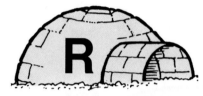 

 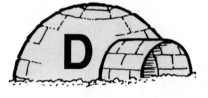 

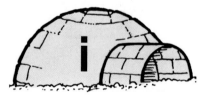 

© Harcourt

Phonics Practice Book

Vowel /i/*i* 55

Name_____

Have children print Ii over Iggy's Igloo. Then ask them to trace and write I and i on the lines.

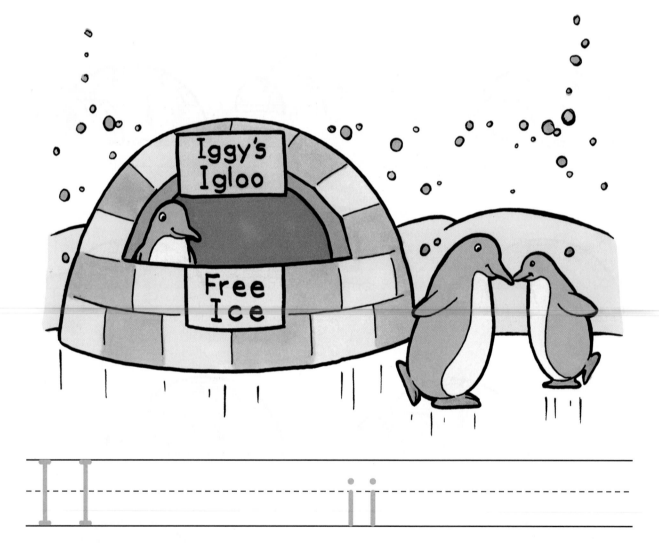

Name_____

Ii

Have children name each picture and color the items whose names begin with the /i/ sound, as in *iguana*.

Name_____

Ii

Ask children to listen for the beginning sound as you say the name of each picture. Have children write I or i on the lines if the picture name begins with the letter Ii.

_I i_		

© Harcourt

Name _____

Say the name of each picture. Then have children circle the letter that stands for its beginning sound.

g   **f**   **a**

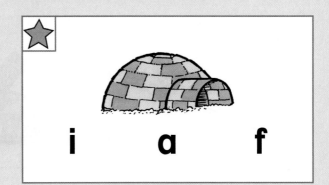

i   **a**   **f**

n   **d**   **f**

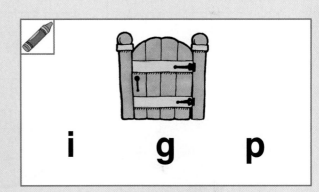

i   **g**   **p**

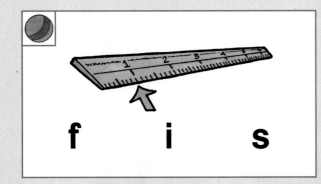

f   **i**   **s**

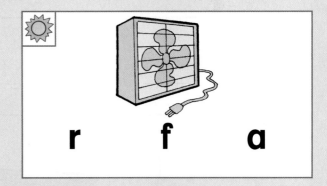

r   **f**   **a**

g   **p**   **c**

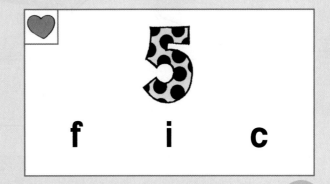

f   **i**   **c**

Name

Say the name of each picture. Then have children write the letter that stands for its beginning sound.

Phonics Practice Book

Name_____

L l

Have children name and trace the letter Ll at the top of the page. Ask them to find and mark the letter Ll in the lamps.

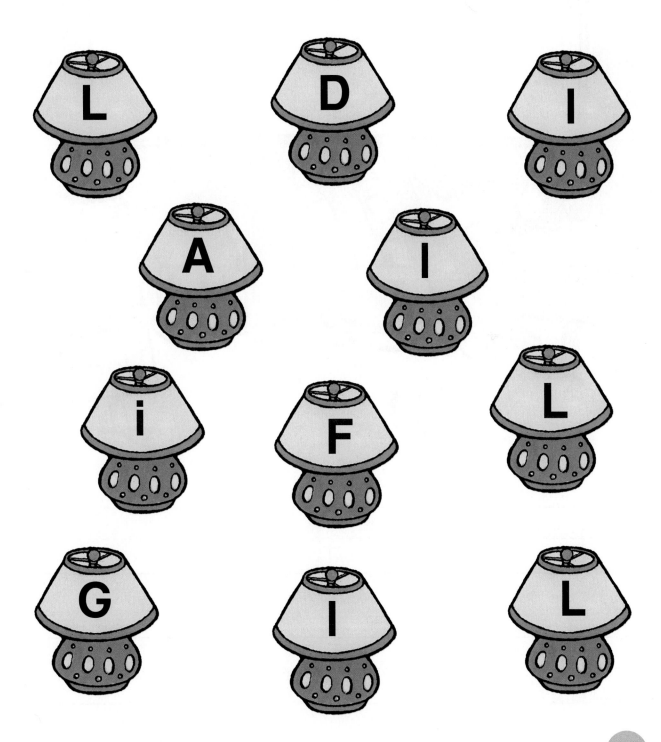

Consonant /l/ **61**

Name_____

Have children print Ll on the zoo sign. Then ask them to trace and write L and l on the lines.

Please Don't Feed the Lions.

Lions

Name _____

LI

Have children name each picture and color the items whose names begin with the /l/ sound, as in *lamb*.

© Harcourt

Name_____

LI

Ask children to listen for the beginning sound as you say the name of each picture. Have children write L or l on the lines if the picture name begins with the letter Ll.

Name _____

Hh

Have children name and trace the letter Hh at the top of the page. Ask them to find and mark the letter Hh in the hearts.

Name_____

© Harcourt

Name _____

Hh

Have children name each picture and color the items whose names begin with the /h/ sound, as in *hippo*.

Phonics Practice Book

Consonant /h/*h* 67

Name_____

Hh

Ask children to listen for the beginning sound as you say the name of each picture. Have children write H or h on the lines if the picture name begins with the letter Hh.

Hh

Phonics Practice Book

Name_____

Say the name of each picture. Then have children circle the letter that stands for its beginning sound.

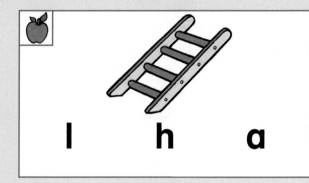

l   h   a

l   f   h

n   h   f

i   h   p

h   i   l

r   l   a

l   h   c

f   l   h

© Harcourt

Phonics Practice Book

Name_____

Say the name of each picture. Then have children write the letter that stands for its beginning sound.

Phonics Practice Book

Name_____

Bb

Have children name and trace the letter Bb at the top of the page. Ask them to find and mark the letter Bb in the beds.

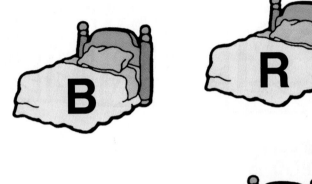

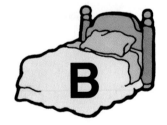

Name_____

BB   bb

BB   bb

© Harcourt

Name _____

Bb

Have children name and trace the letter Bb at the top of the page. Ask them to find and mark the letter Bb in the beds.

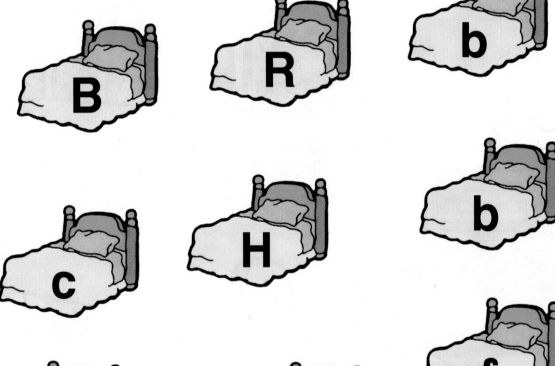

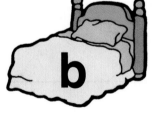

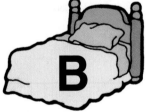

© Harcourt

Name_____

Have children print Bb on the side of the bus. Then ask
them to trace and write B and b on the lines.

BB   bb

BB   bb

© Harcourt

Name_____

Bb

Have children name each picture and color the items whose names begin with the /b/ sound, as in *bear*.

Bb

Ask children to listen for the beginning sound as you say the name of each picture. Have children write B or b on the lines if the picture name begins with the letter Bb.

Bb

Consonant /b/b

© Harcourt

Phonics Practice Book

Name_____

Kk

Have children name and trace the letter Kk at the top of the page. Ask them to find and mark the letter Kk in the kites.

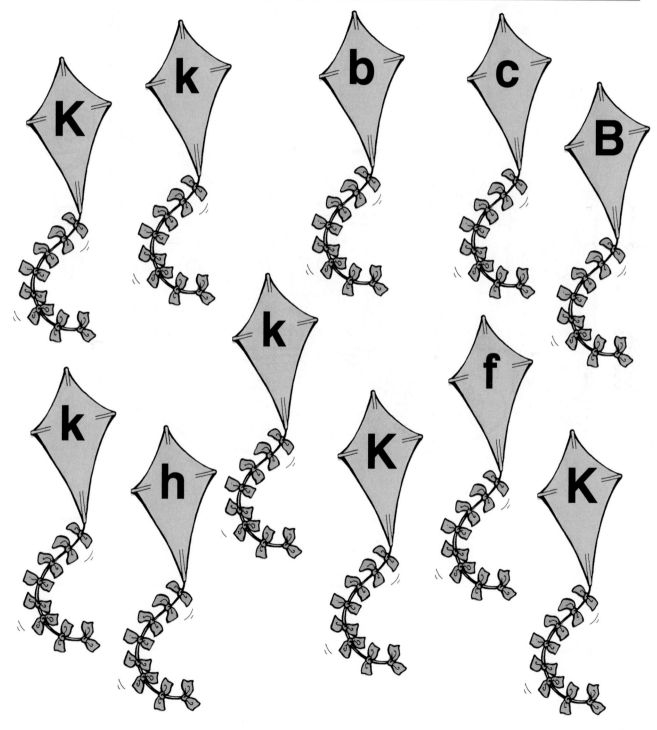

© Harcourt

Name _____

Have children print Kk over the kitchen. Then ask them to trace and write K and k on the lines.

KK   kk

KK   kk

© Harcourt

Name _____

Kk

Have children name each picture and color the items whose names begin with the /k/ sound, as in *kangaroo*.

Kk

Ask children to listen for the beginning sound as you say the name of each picture. Have children write K or k on the lines if the picture name begins with the letter Kk.

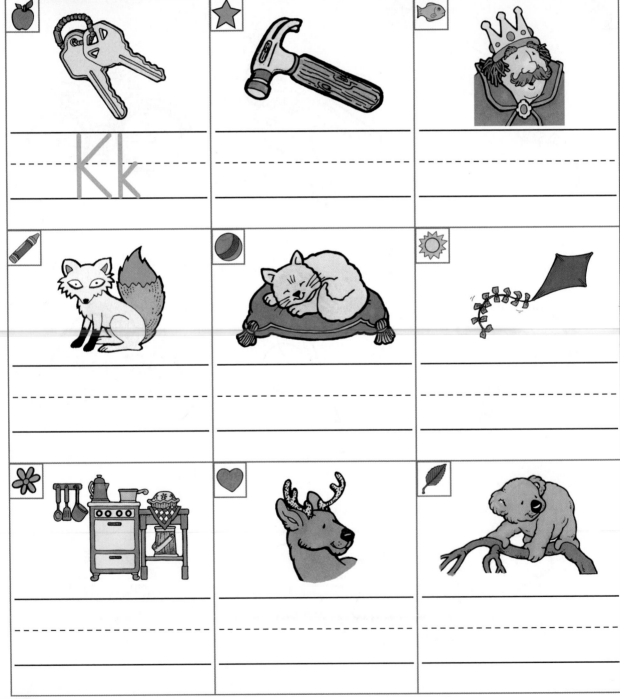

Name _____

© Harcourt

Have children name and trace the letter Oo at the top of the page. Ask them to find and mark the letter Oo in the octopuses.

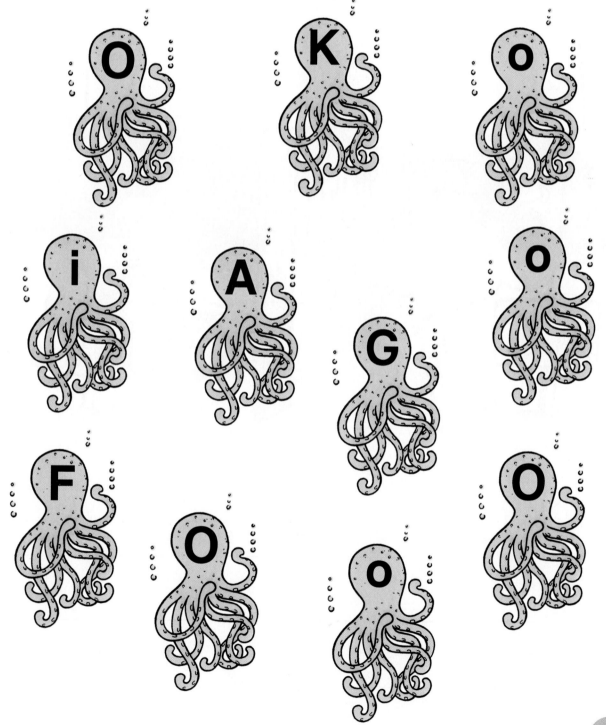

Vowel *o*   79

Name_____

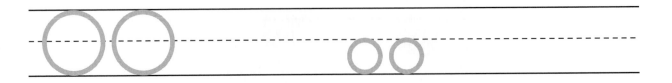

Name_____

Oo

Have children name each picture and color the items whose names begin with the /o/ sound, as in *octopus*.

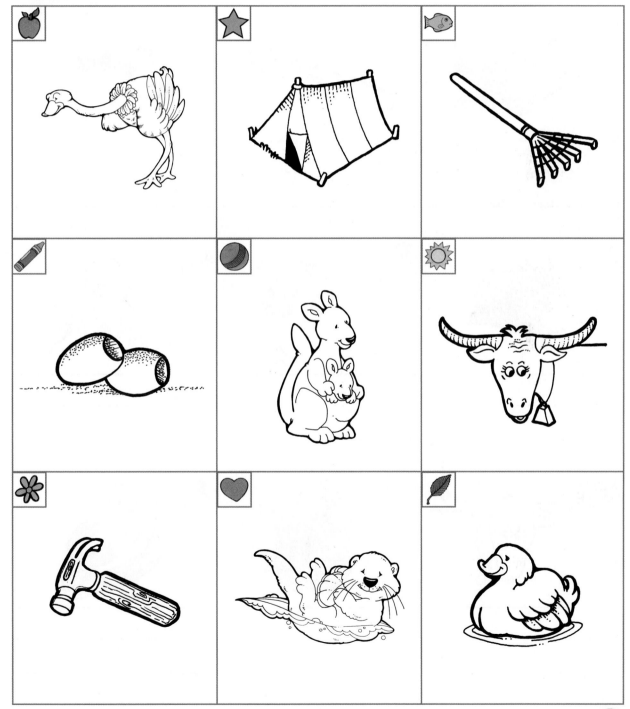

Name_____

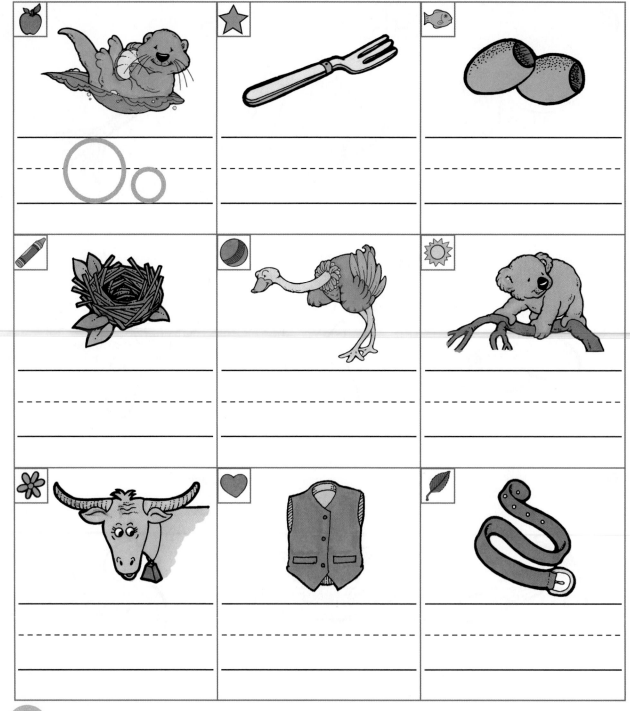

Oo

Ask children to listen for the beginning sound as you say the name of each picture.
Have children write O or o on the lines if the picture name begins with the letter Oo.

Phonics Practice Book

Name _____

Say the name of each picture. Then have children circle the letter that stands for its beginning sound.

b　　**h**　　**k**

o　　**f**　　**b**

b　　**o**　　**k**

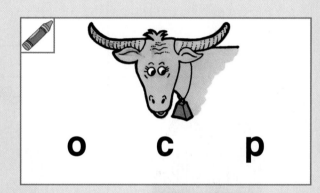

o　　**c**　　**p**

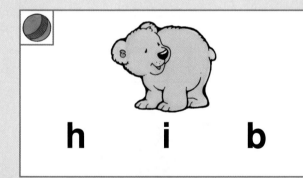

h　　**i**　　**b**

b　　**l**　　**o**

o　　**h**　　**k**

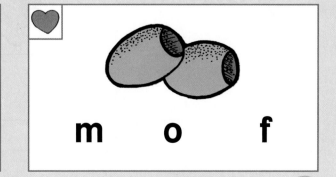

m　　**o**　　**f**

Say the name of each picture. Then have children write
the letter that stands for its beginning sound.

Name _____

Ww

Have children name and trace the letter Ww at the top of the page. Ask them to find and mark the letter Ww in the wagons.

Name _____

Ww

Ask children to listen for the beginning sound as you say the name of each picture. Have children write W or w on the lines if the picture name begins with the letter Ww.

Consonant /w/w

Phonics Practice Book

Name _____

Have children name and trace the letter Xx at the top of the page. Ask them to find and mark the letter Xx in the boxes.

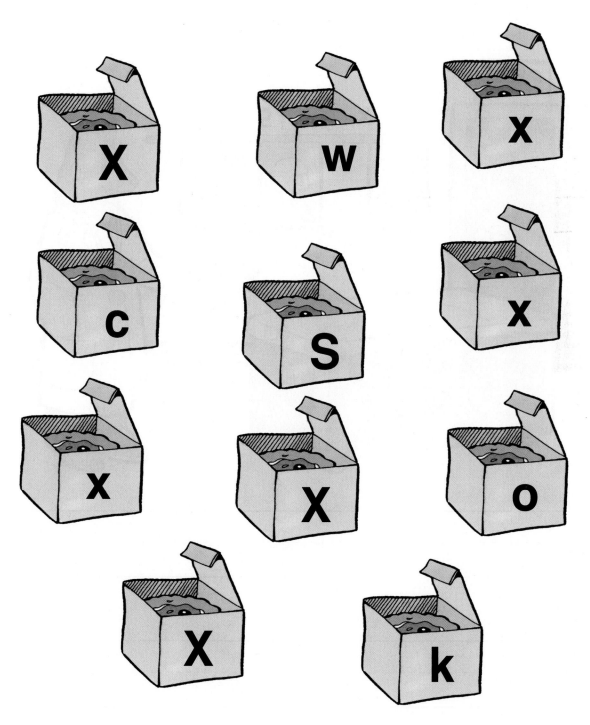

Consonant /ks/x **89**

Name

Phonics Practice Book

Name_____

Xx

Have children name each picture and color the items whose names begin or end with the /ks/ sound, as in *fox* and *x-ray*.

© Harcourt

Name _____

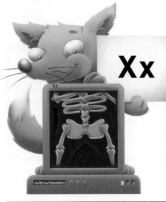

Xx

Ask children to listen for the beginning sound as you say the name of each picture. Have children write X or x on the lines if the picture name begins or ends with the letter Xx.

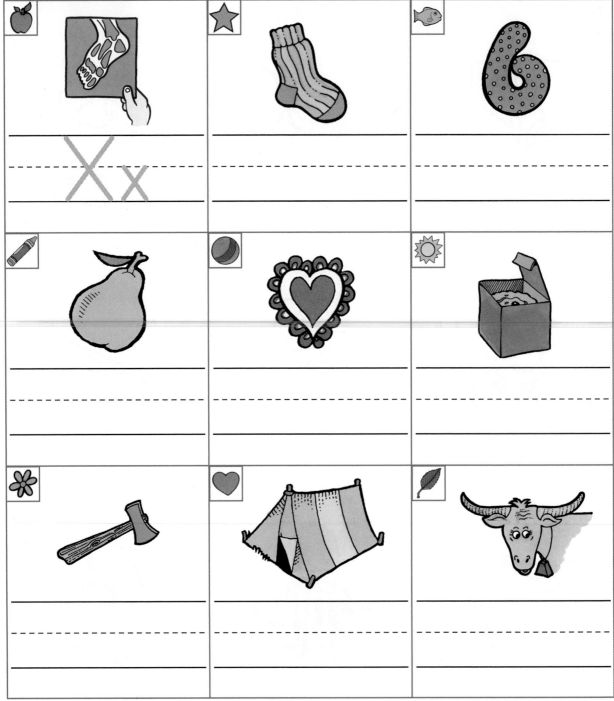

© Harcourt

Say the name of each picture. Then have children circle the letter that stands for its beginning or ending sound.

b   w   x

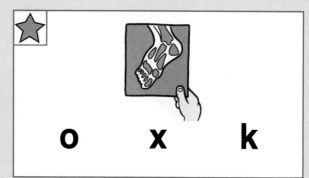

o   x   k

x   l   k

p   c   x

h   w   b

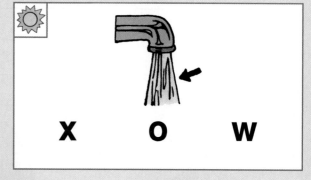

x   o   w

a   h   x

w   m   f

© Harcourt

Name_____

Say the name of each picture. Then have children write the letter that stands for its beginning or ending sound.

© Harcourt

Name_____

Vv

V

W

v

X

o

v

v

V

k

V

p

Name_____

Have children print Vv on the banner. Then ask them to trace and write V and v on the lines.

Consonant /v/v

Phonics Practice Book

© Harcourt

V v

Have children name and trace the letter Vv at the top of the page. Ask them to find and mark the letter Vv in the vans.

Name

Happy Valentine's Day

I Love Val

V V   v v

V V   v v

Name _____

Vv

Have children name each picture and color the items whose names begin with the /v/ sound, as in *vulture*.

Vv

Ask children to listen for the beginning sound as you say the name of each picture. Have children write V or v on the lines if the picture name begins with the letter Vv.

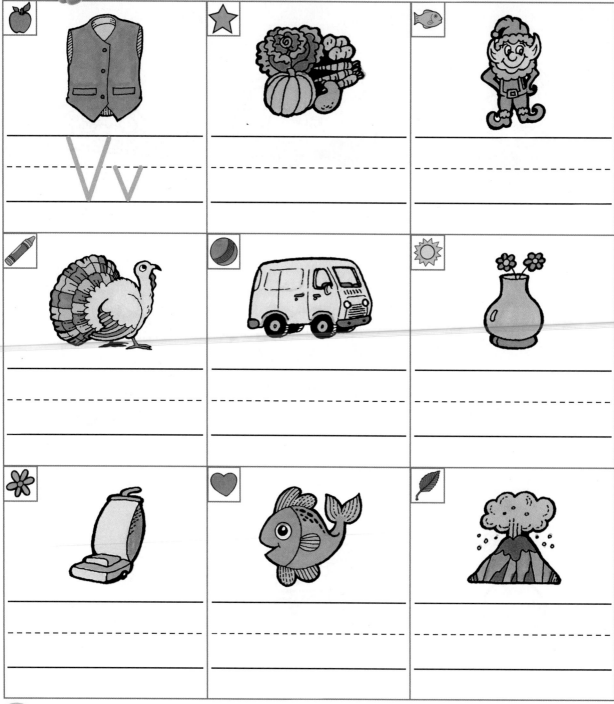

Name _____

Vv

Have children name each picture and color the items whose names begin with the /v/ sound, as in *vulture*.

Name_____

Vv

Ask children to listen for the beginning sound as you say the name of each picture. Have children write V or v on the lines if the picture name begins with the letter Vv.

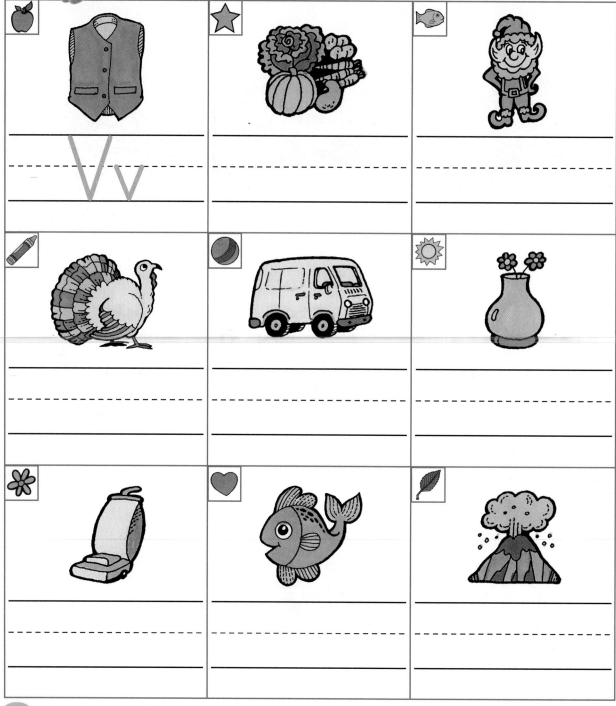

Name_____

Jj

Have children name and trace the letter Jj at the top of the page. Ask them to find and mark the letter Jj in the jars.

Name_____

Have children print Jj on the store roof. Then ask them
to trace and write J and j on the lines.

Jack's Toys

Jets
$10

JJ   jj

JJ   jj

Name _____

Jj

Have children name each picture and color the items whose names begin with the / j / sound, as in *jellyfish*.

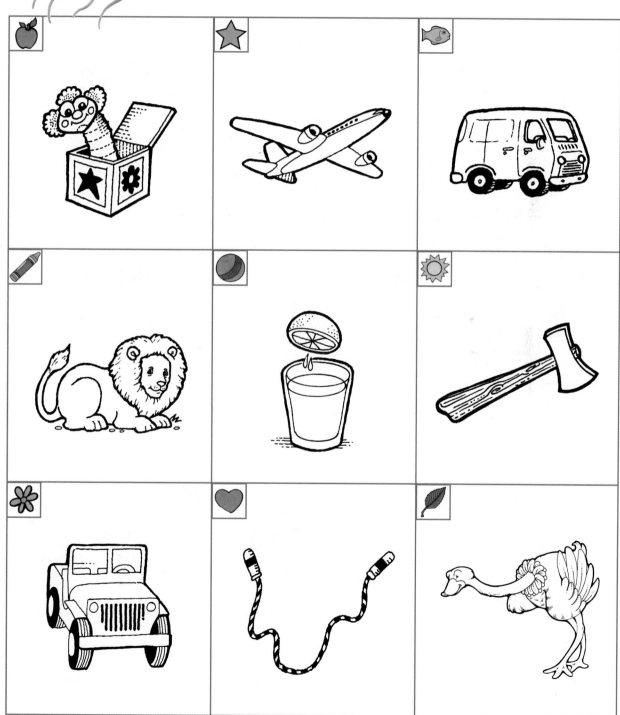

Phonics Practice Book

Consonant /j/*j*   **101**

Name_____

Jj

Ask children to listen for the beginning sound as you say the name of each picture. Have children write J or j on the lines if the picture name begins with the letter Jj.

Name _____

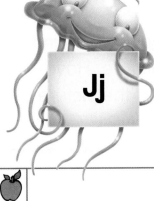

Jj

Have children name each picture and color the items whose names begin with the /j/ sound, as in *jellyfish*.

Name

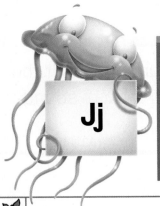

Jj

Ask children to listen for the beginning sound as you say the name of each picture. Have children write J or j on the lines if the picture name begins with the letter Jj.

Ee

Have children name and trace the letter Ee at the top of the page. Ask them to find and mark the letter Ee in the eggs.

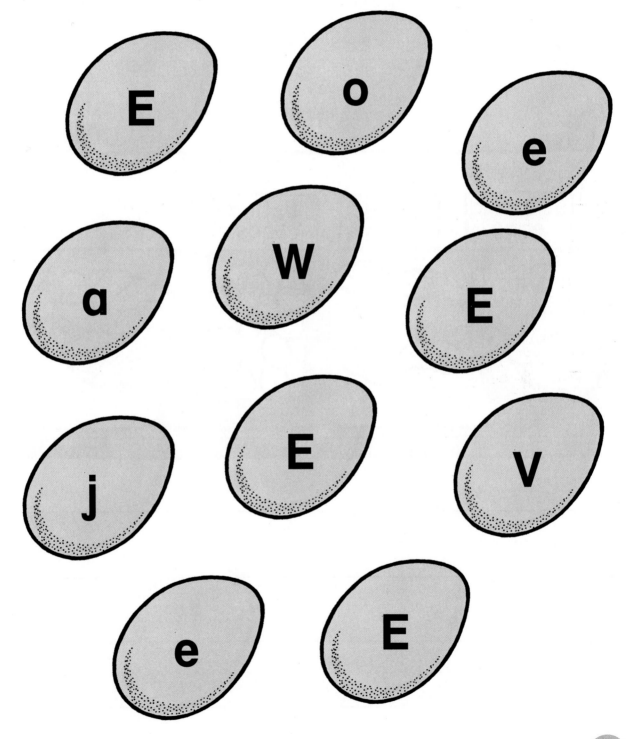

Have children print Ee on the sign in the cafeteria. Then ask them to trace and write E and e on the lines.

EE   ee

EE   ee

© Harcourt

Name _____

Ee

Have children name each picture and color the items whose names begin with the /e/ sound, as in *elephant*.

Name_____

Ask children to listen for the beginning sound as you say the name of each picture. Have children write E or e on the lines if the picture name begins with the letter Ee.

Say the name of each picture. Then have children circle the letter that stands for its beginning sound.

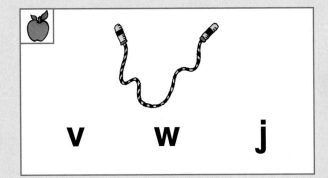

v   w   j

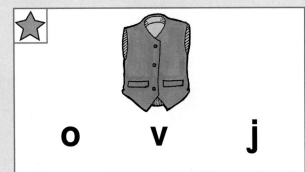

o   v   j

j   e   v

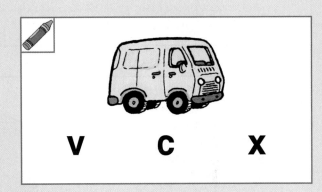

v   c   x

e   v   b

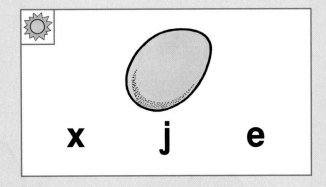

x   j   e

a   h   j

m   j   f

Name_____

Say the name of each picture. Then have children write the letter that stands for its beginning sound.

Phonics Practice Book

Name_____

Yy

Have children name and trace the letter Yy at the top of the page. Ask them to find and mark the letter Yy in the yo-yos.

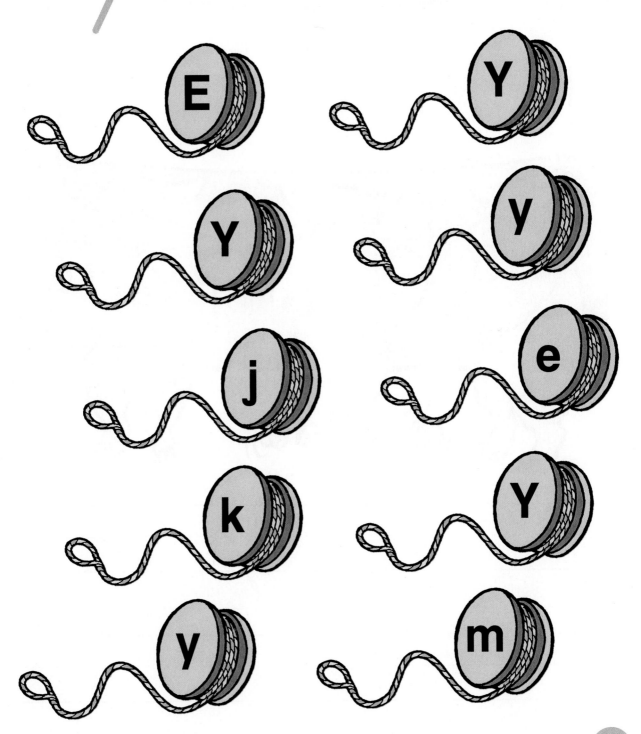

Name

Have children print Yy on the banner. Then ask them to trace and write Y and y on the lines.

Yes!

Y Y

y y

Y Y

y y

© Harcourt

Name_____

Yy

Have children name each picture and color the items whose names begin with the /y/ sound, as in *yak*.

Yy

Ask children to listen for the beginning sound as you say the name of each picture. Have children write Y or y on the lines if the picture name begins with the letter Yy.

_____ Yy _____

_____

_____

_____

_____

_____

_____

_____

_____

Zz

Have children name and trace the letter Zz at the top of the page. Ask them to find and mark the letter Zz in the zebras.

Have children print Zz on the zoo sign. Then ask them to trace and write Z and z on the lines.

Zebras

ZOO
Tickets
$2

© Harcourt

Name _____

Zz

Have children name each picture and color the items whose names begin with the /z/ sound, as in *zebra*.

© Harcourt

Name_____

Ask children to listen for the beginning sound as you say the name of each picture. Have children write Z or z on the lines if the picture name begins with the letter Zz.

Phonics Practice Book

© Harcourt

Name_____

Say the name of each picture. Then have children circle the letter that stands for its beginning sound.

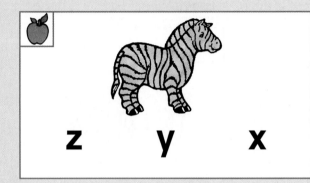

z   y   x

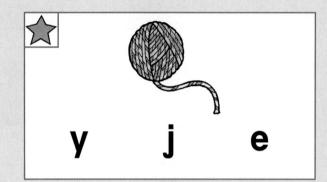

y   j   e

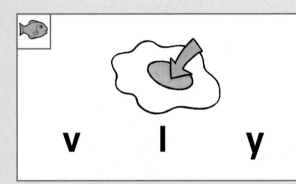

v   l   y

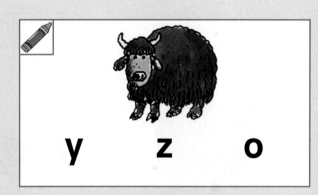

y   z   o

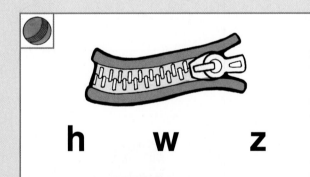

h   w   z

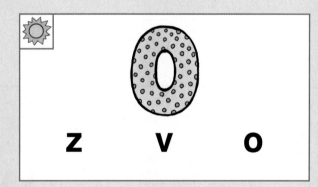

z   v   o

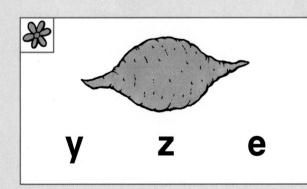

y   z   e

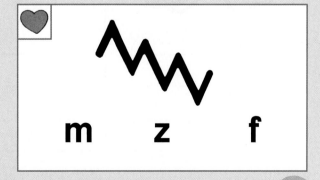

m   z   f

Name_____

Say the name of each picture. Then have children
write the letter that stands for its beginning sound.

© Harcourt

Qq

Have children name and trace the letter Qq at the top of the page. Ask them to find and mark the letter Qq in the quilts.

Have children print Qq above the queen. Then ask them to trace and write Q and q on the lines.

Long Live
the
Queen!

Q Q   q q

Q Q   q q

Name _____

Qq

Have children name each picture and color the items whose names begin with the /kw/ sound, as in *quail*.

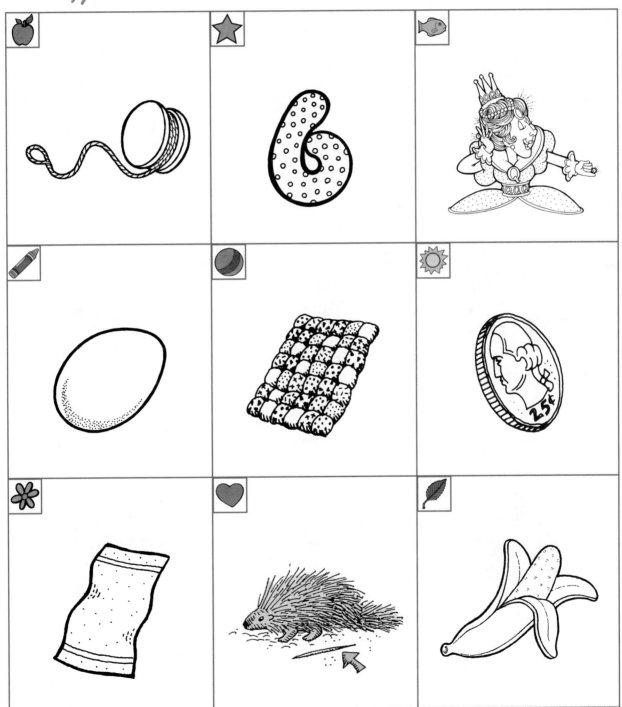

Phonics Practice Book

Consonant /kw/ *q* 121

Name _____

Qq

Ask children to listen for the beginning sound as you say the name of each picture. Have children write Q or q on the lines if the picture name begins with the letter Qq.

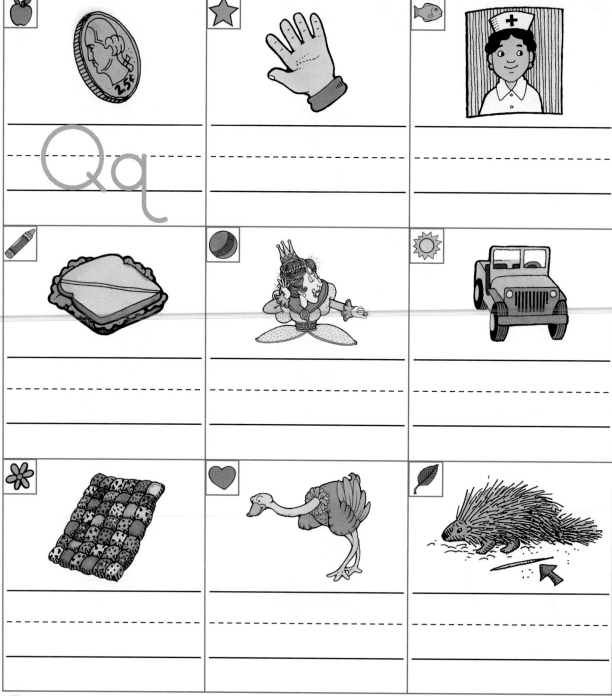

Phonics Practice Book

Name_____

Qq

Have children name each picture and color the items whose names begin with the /kw/ sound, as in *quail*.

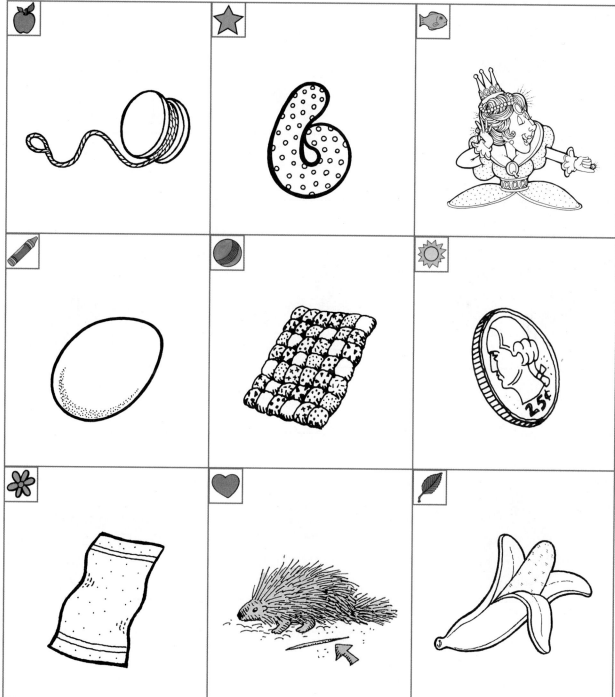

Name _____

Ask children to listen for the beginning sound as you say the name of each picture. Have children write Q or q on the lines if the picture name begins with the letter Qq.

Qq

© Harcourt

Name_____

Uu

Have children name and trace the letter Uu at the top of the page. Ask them to find and mark the letter Uu in the umbrellas.

© Harcourt

Phonics Practice Book

Vowel *u* 123

Have children print Uu on the sign. Then ask them to trace and write U and u on the lines.

Umbrellas for Sale

Phonics Practice Book

Name_____

Uu

Have children name each picture and color the items whose names begin with the /u/ sound, as in *umbrella*.

© Harcourt

Name_____

Uu

Ask children to listen for the beginning sound as you say the name of each picture. Have children write U or u on the lines if the picture name begins with the letter Uu.

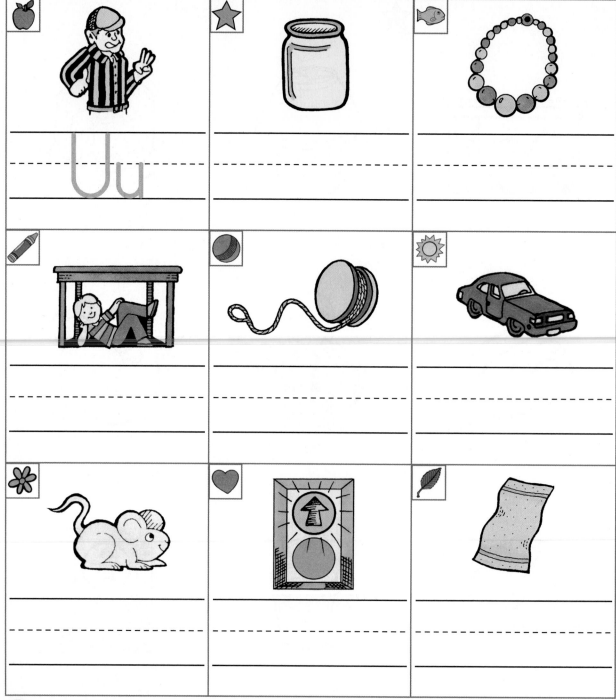

Vowel /u/u

Name _____

Uu

Have children name each picture and color the items whose names begin with the /u/ sound, as in *umbrella*.

Name

Uu

Ask children to listen for the beginning sound as you say the name of each picture. Have children write U or u on the lines if the picture name begins with the letter Uu.

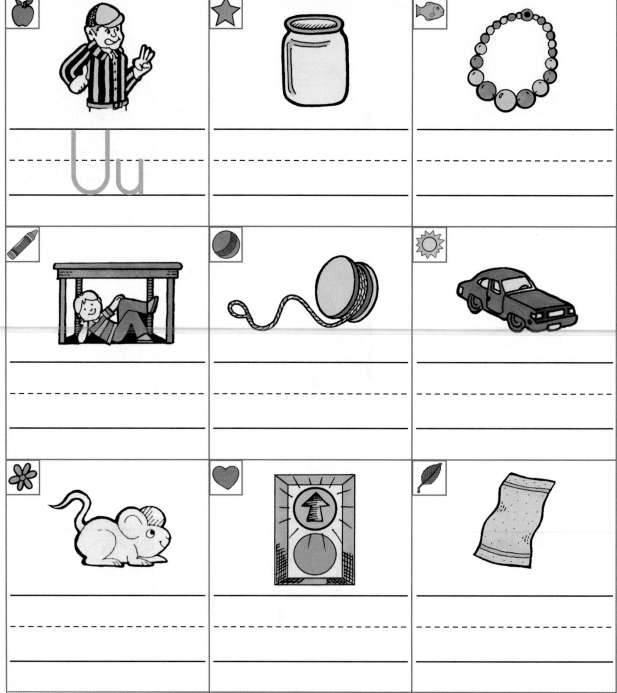

Vowel /u/u

© Harcourt

Name _____

Say the name of each picture. Then have children circle the letter that stands for its beginning sound.

u   q   z

m   u   q

v   q   y

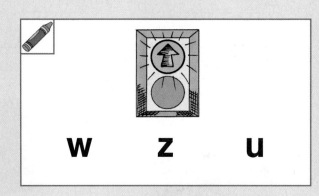

w   z   u

h   j   u

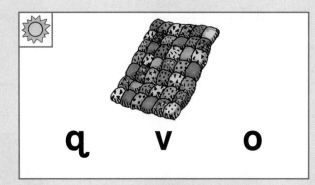

q   v   o

y   q   u

u   z   f

Name _____

Say the name of each picture. Then have children write the letter that stands for its beginning sound.

© Harcourt

Phonics Practice Book

My
Alphabet
Book

_____

Name

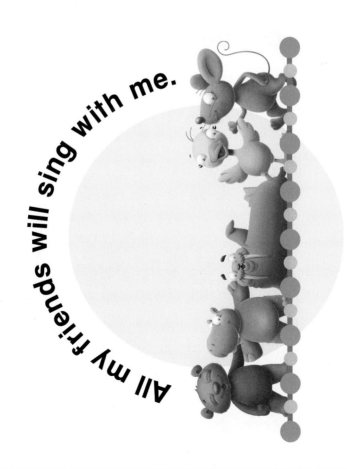

All my friends will sing with me.

Directions: Help your child cut out and fold up the book.

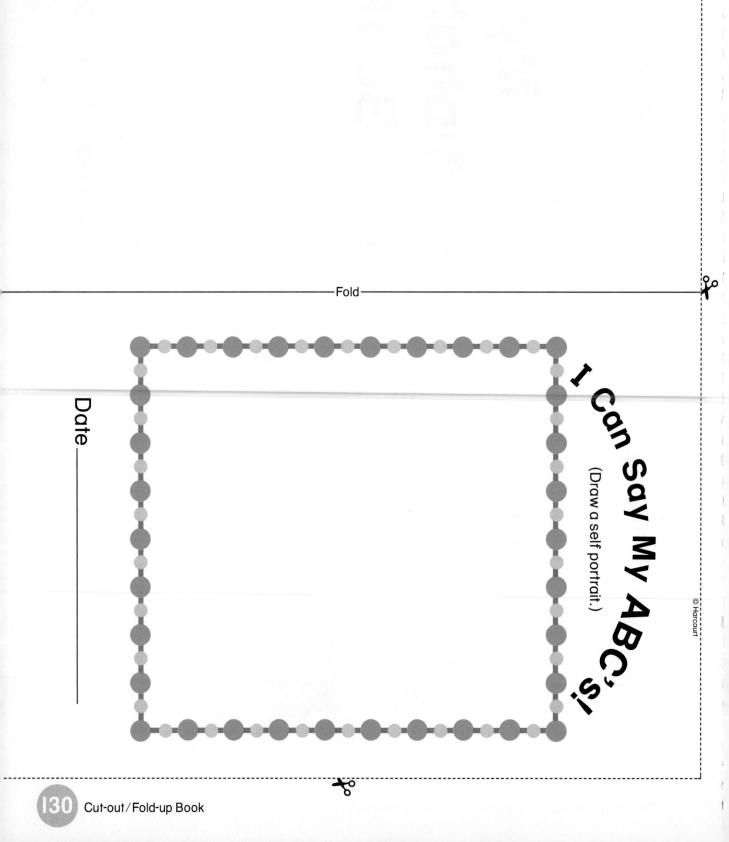

Fold

Date —————

I Can Say My ABC's!

(Draw a self portrait.)

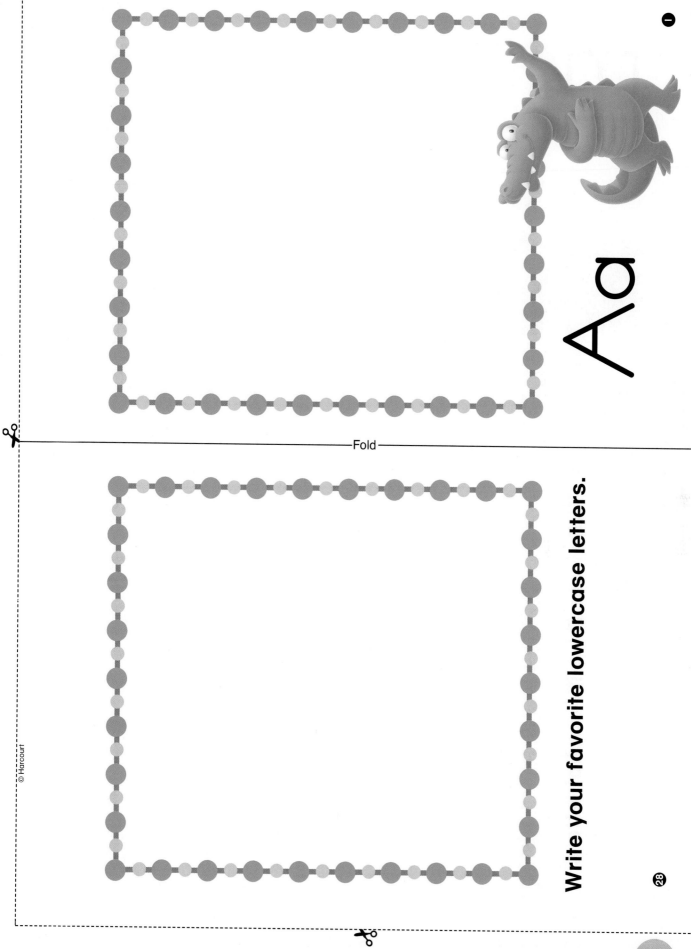

Aa

Fold

Write your favorite lowercase letters.

28

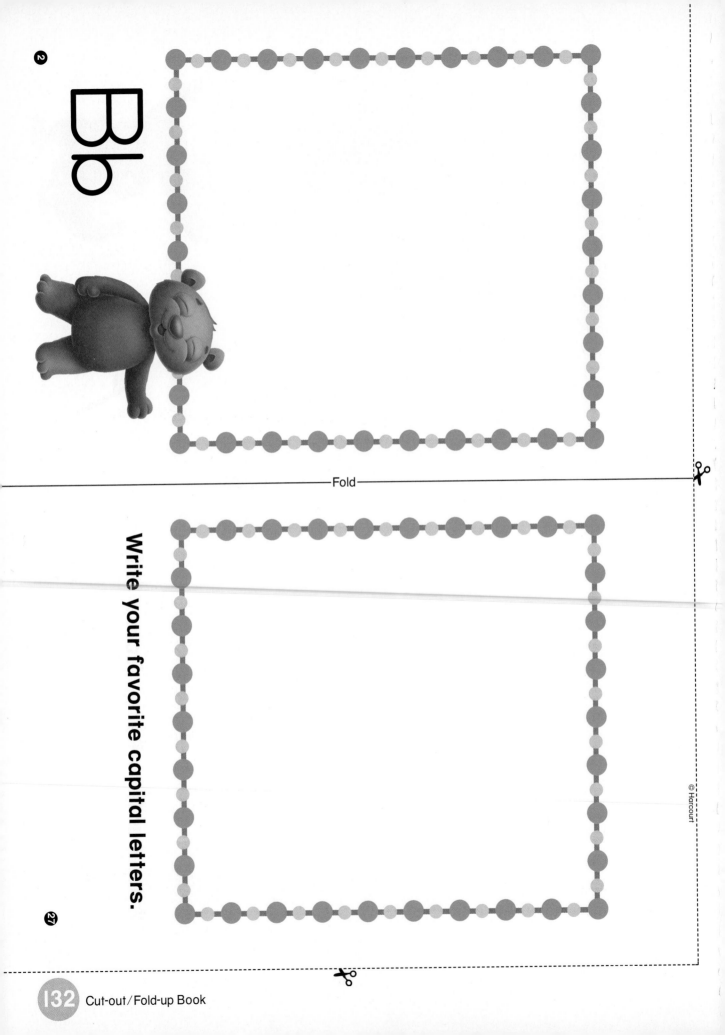

Bb

—Fold—

Write your favorite capital letters.

Cc

Fold

Zz

26

4

Dd

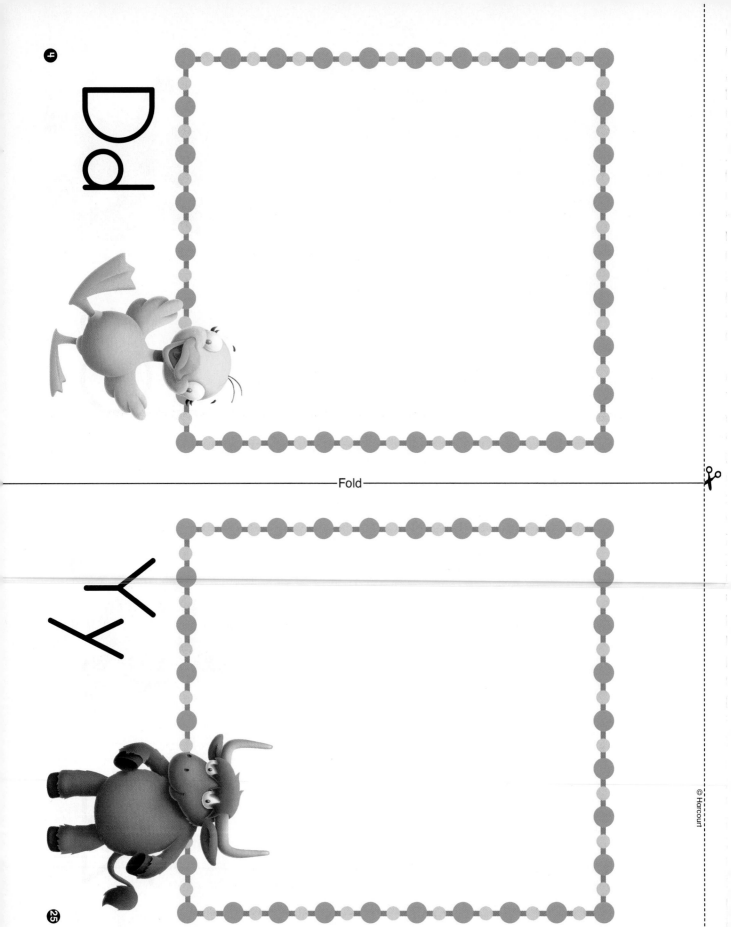

————————————Fold————————————

Yy

25

Ee

— Fold —

Xx

㉔

6

Ff

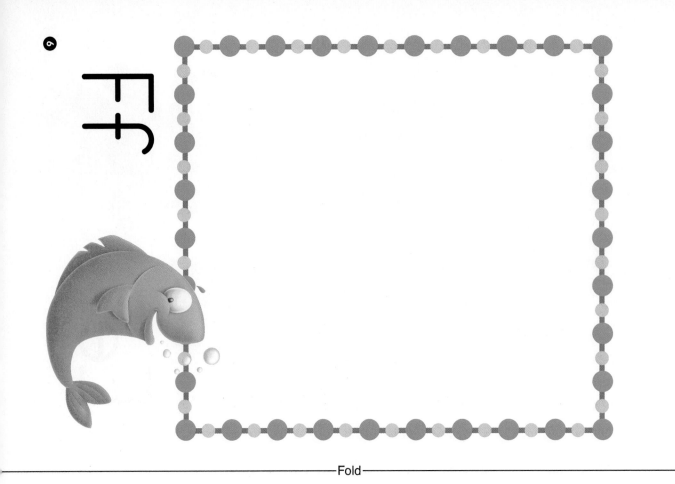

———Fold———

Ww

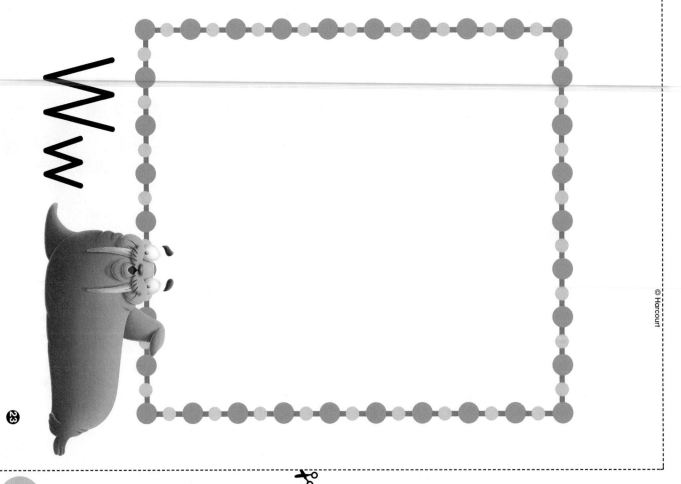

23

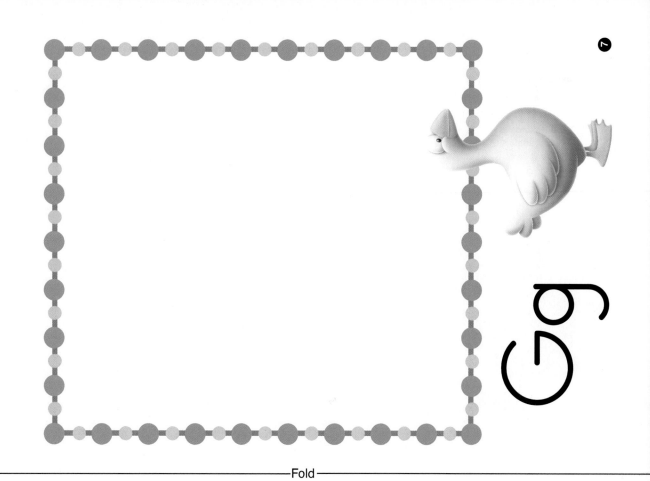

Gg

⑦

Fold

Vv

㉒

8

Hh

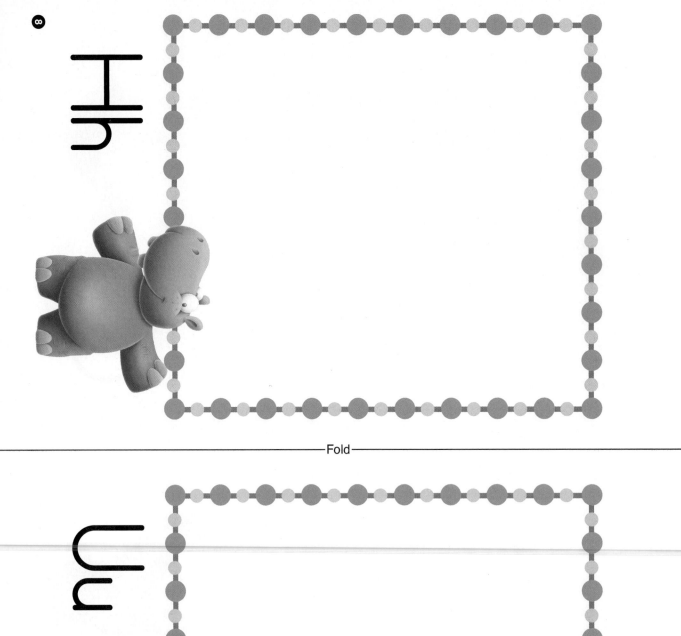

---Fold---

Uu

20

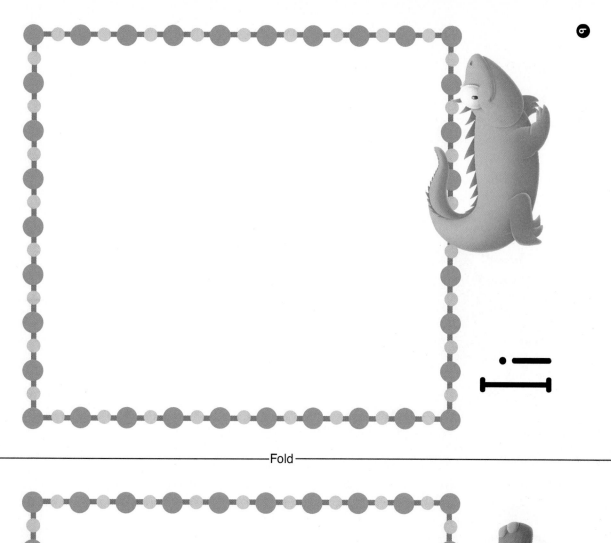

Ii

Fold

Tt

20

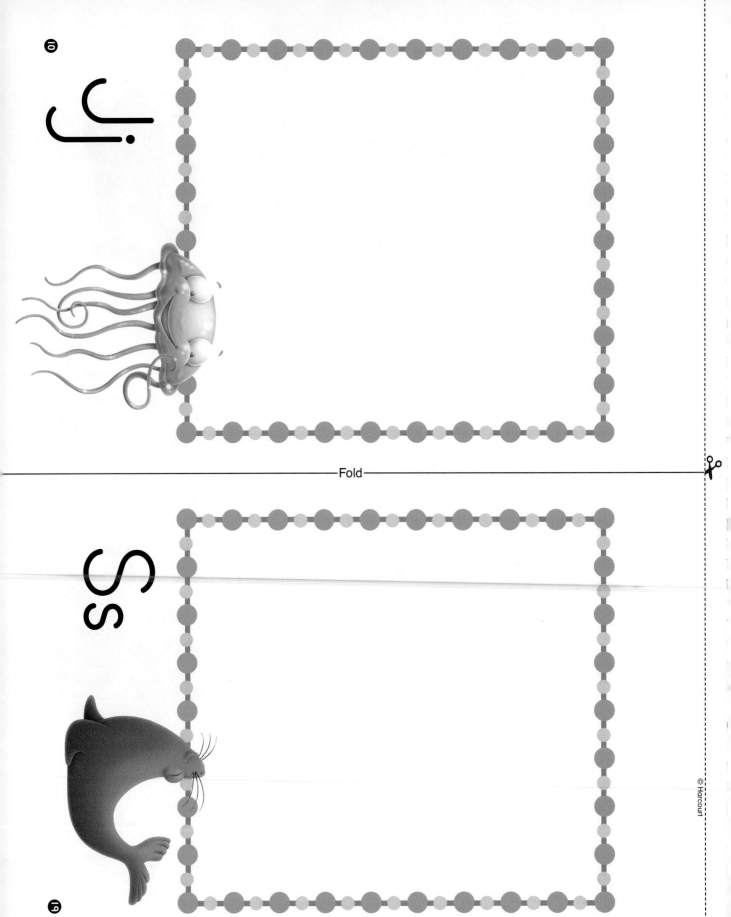

Jj

Ss

Fold

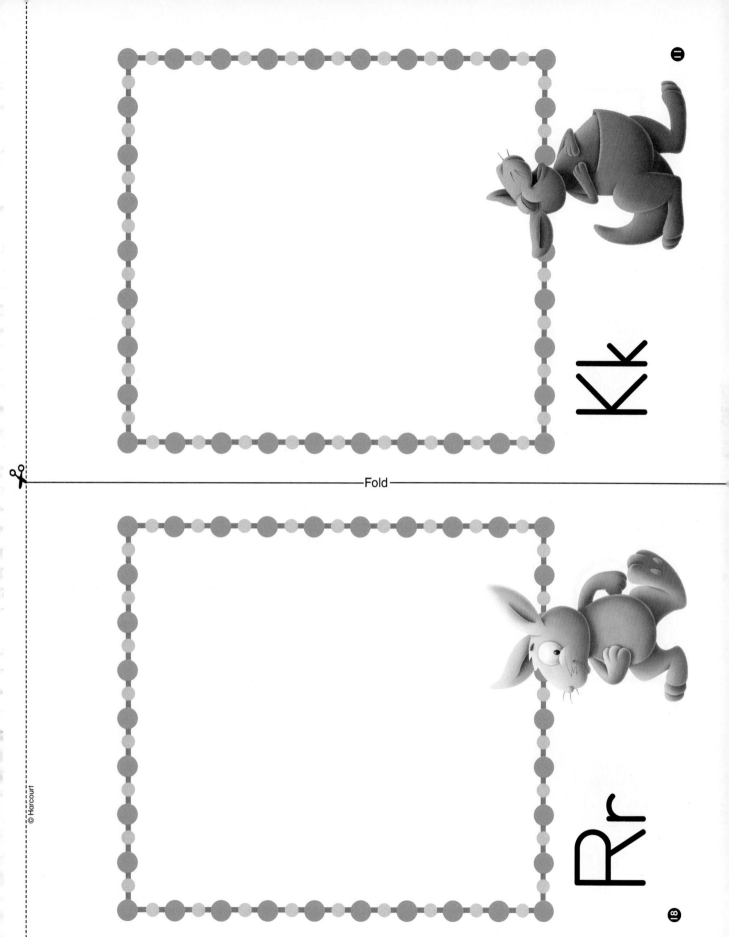

Kk

11

—— Fold ——

Rr

18

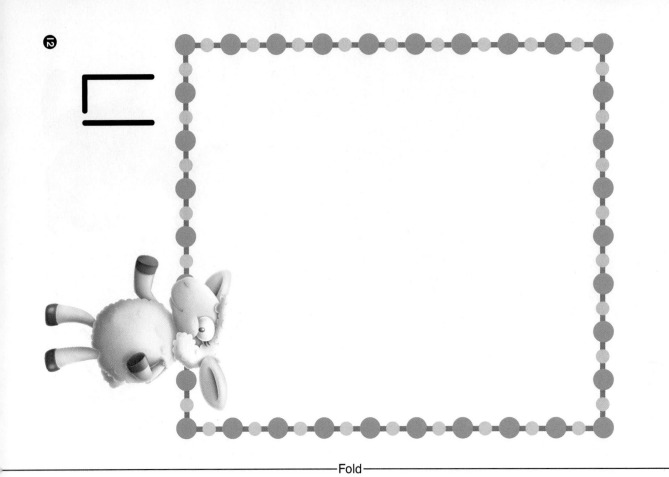

Ll

12

Fold

Qq

17

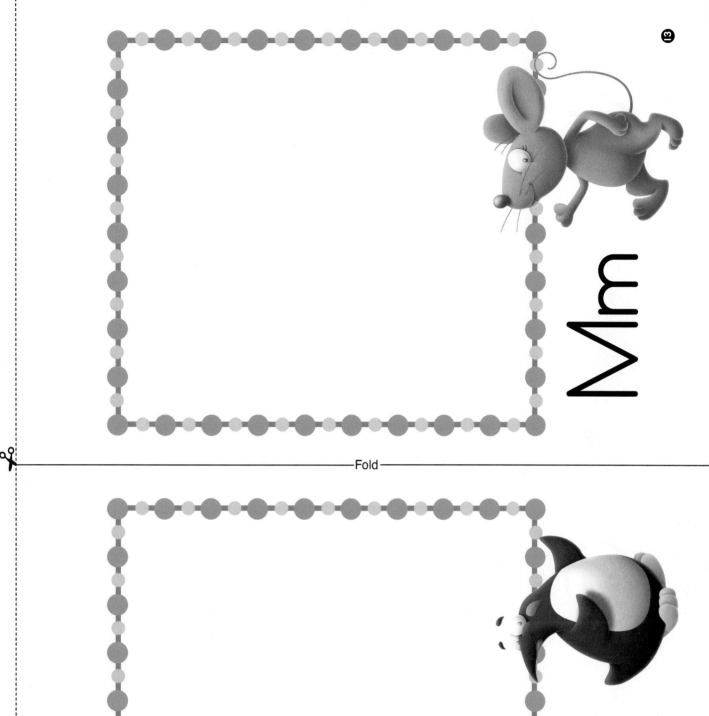

Mm

⑬

Fold

Pp

⑯

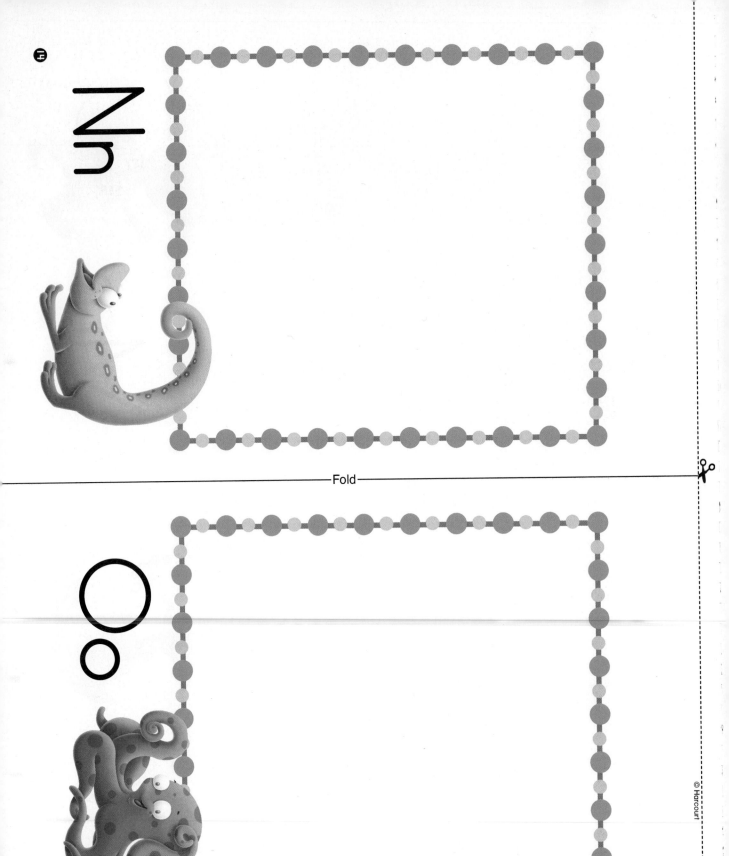

Nn

— Fold —

Oo